PLANTS AND DESIGN

What would a garden be without plants? They define and implement our design, challenge our horticultural expertise, and offer us beauty, protection, and shade. As their leaves photosynthesize, they exchange atmospheric carbon dioxide for life-giving oxygen. In many gardens, plants even provide fresh, healthy food. Watching them thrive under our care is one of the most satisfying aspects of gardening.

If you think of your garden as a painting, all the plants you grow — with their infinite combinations of height, shape and texture — form the brushstrokes, the colour, the lines, and the mass.

On the following pages, we'll look at some hardy shade or specimen trees before exploring how to design with the smaller flowering trees and large shrubs. Then we'll move to the understory layer: the smaller shrubs, woody vines, clematis, roses, perennials, ferns, grasses, bulbs, and annuals that offer versatility in our gardens. At the end of the book, you'll find listings of plants for particular growing conditions and design uses.

DESIGNING WITH PLANTS

Plants exist in well-ordered arrangements of height, from the tree canopy to the understory layer of shrubs, grasses, and flowers. Planning your garden around the canopy and understory will help you fulfil some of the requirements of good design. The plants will be layered, providing visual interest. There will be a contrast of leaf colour and texture and heights will vary. The upper canopy is not always defined by towering trees; if your garden is tiny, your canopy may be a single small tree, such as a flowering crab, underplanted with dwarf Japanese yews, and groundcover, such as ajuga, or low-growing perennials. The canopy might instead be a specimen tree, like a Japanese maple, or two columnar trees that frame a walkway and formalize your garden. Plants can be used to create structure and style. For instance, a formal design will use plants such as boxwood, English ivy, and conical evergreens.

PLANT NAMES

In some spots in this book, and in the plant lists that follow, we've provided you with both the common names and botanical names of plants. Although those tongue-twisting botanical names may be hard to get used to, they're valuable to have when you visit a nursery or garden centre or browse through catalogues and books. Many plants have different common names depending on the part of the country you live in, so the only way to be sure you're getting what you want is to check the botanical name.

• The first word (for example, *Dicentra*) is the genus name and is italicized. A genus is group of plants that are closely related, like members of a family, and have one or more species. Bleeding hearts belong to the genus *Dicentra*; crabapples belong to the genus *Malus*.

• The second word is the species name, also italicized, and describes the plant. *Dicentra spectabilis* is the plant we know by its common name of bleeding heart. Sometimes there is a third italicized name, which further describes the plant.

• A name enclosed in single quotes — 'Purple Sensation' or 'Arctic Queen', for example — signifies a cultivated variety (also called cultivar). *Dicentra spectabilis* 'Alba' is a bleeding heart that has a white flower; "alba" means white.

Species names can be applied to more than one genus. For example, *rubrum* or *rubra*, which means red, is found in *Acer rubrum* (red maple), as well as in *Quercus rubra* (red oak).

PUTTING IT ALL TOGETHER

Because the canopy is such an important part of the design, we're starting with trees. And when you're planting, that's where you should start, too. Just as a painter starts with the background and fills in the details last, a gardener should first plant the larger elements that will act as background to the colourful and beautiful flowers, smaller shrubs, and vines that will fill in the picture.

When you plant, be guided by the following hierarchy. Take into account the scale of your surroundings — not every garden needs or can accommodate a towering oak — and the width of your planting bed. In small gardens, the canopy is likely to start with shrubs.

The planting sequence to follow is:

1. canopy level: trees, tall multi-stemmed shrubs
2. mid-level: shorter shrubs, tall perennials and annuals, vines
3. lower level: dwarf shrubs, perennials and annuals, groundcovers

When buying any of the above kinds of plant material, consider:

- flowering or leafing-out time
- mature height and spread
- light, soil, and moisture requirements

In a garden spacious enough to accommodate it, a large tree provides a magestic canopy.

SPARE THAT TREE!

Every time you add or remove any plant, you change the landscape, and when that plant is a tree, the change can be profound. Before you start calling in tree-removal experts:

- be sure that the problem is the tree and not the plantings around it
- assess whether the tree can be improved by judicious pruning
- carefully check what the impact of removing the tree will be — for example, where will sunshine fall, what views will be opened up?

PLANT VOCABULARY

Throughout this book, and when you go to buy plants, you'll come across terms to describe various types of plants. Here's a basic vocabulary with definitions.

EVERGREEN: describes plants whose leaves or needles remain green and functioning throughout the year

BROAD-LEAF EVERGREEN: woody plants that keep all or part of their foliage throughout the year; foliage often changes colour from season to season; they produce flowers and fruit

DECIDUOUS: usually used to describe trees that shed their leaves in winter

TALL TREE: tree with mature height between 9 and 24 m (30 and 80 feet)

MID-SIZE TREE: tree with mature height up to 9 m (30 feet)

SHRUB: compared to a tree, a low-growing woody plant, usually having several stems, not a single trunk

MULTI-STEMMED: describes most shrubs and a few trees; has more than one stem at its base

SPECIMEN PLANT: a plant kept separate from others; given a prominent position because of its attractive form; used as a focal point

STANDARD: tree, shrub, or plant grown on a single stem to which it is grafted; height ranges from 1 to 1.5 m (3 to 5 feet)

PERENNIAL: plant that lives more than two years or three seasons and flowers every year; the foliage usually dies down in the winter, but the roots remain living; has a specific flowering period, usually from two to six weeks

BIENNIAL: plant that completes its life cycle in two years: seed is sown the first year, flowers or fruit are produced the next year

ANNUAL: a plant that completes its life cycle in one year, from germination to death; most are not frost-tolerant; flower continuously throughout season

GROUNDCOVER: low-growing plants often used to suppress weeds or prevent erosion; a good alternative to grass; provides beautiful texture; low maintenance

TREES

P lanting a tree is an expression of hope, an investment in the future of the garden.

Ideally, every garden, even a small one, should have at least one tree — just look for a tree that is suitable in scale to your garden. Only a large or rural property has the space needed for a massive oak, elm, sugar maple, or beech. But many wonderful trees are well-suited to form the canopy of an urban residential garden.

- Blue beech (also known as American hornbeam), yellowwood with its scented spring flowers, seedless varieties of green ash (avoid the species, which is a messy tree), ironwood, and the larger service-berries are all native North American trees that have a place in the garden.

- One of the best garden trees is the callery pear, with white spring blossoms and glossy foliage. It's useful in a shrub border, as a lawn specimen, or wherever a vertical accent is needed.

- If you like elegant shapes and fine foliage, the katsura tree has delicate, heart-shaped leaves and tiered branches.

- Ginkgos, the oldest tree known, seems serenely at home in a Japanese landscape. A columnar form of the ginkgo and other narrowly upright trees like the columnar English oak, and Siberian crabapple are useful for small gardens.

- Weeping or cascading trees like the weeping mulberry, 'Kiku-Shidare' Japanese cherry, and 'Red Jade' or 'Cheal' crabapple look especially graceful when their branches are draped over a pond. Isolate a weeping tree from other trees and shrubs so its form can be better appreciated.

TIPS FOR CHOOSING AND PLANTING TREES

- Because proportion is important in the garden, confirm the mature height and spread of the new plant. The tree you buy will be much smaller than its mature height.

- Don't plant a tree where it will grow into utility lines. The tree will be pruned by the utility company to accommodate its lines, which usually results in a misshapen crown.

- Use the information about the tree's shape and mature spread to determine how close other plants can be to the tree. A plant with a pyramidal shape will not allow for umderplanting, since the widest part will be at its base.

An enticing sunlit view can be glimpsed beyond the shaded garden.

SHRUBS

There probably isn't a more useful or adaptable group of plants in your garden than flowering shrubs. Whether massed with other shrubs in a woodland, interspersed with annuals and perennials in a mixed border, used as lawn specimens to flank a path, or positioned to screen an eyesore, shrubs are invaluable.

- The shrub season begins in late winter or early spring with the evergreen heathers; where hardy, they're perfect in a rock garden with species tulips. Golden forsythia follows. It's a shrub that needs room to extend its lovely branches — don't shear it into a rigid shape. Give it space and underplant it with daffodils, scilla, and early blue-flowered pulmonaria.

- Potentilla is one of our favourite shrubs. Not only is it hardy and extremely drought-tolerant but it has lots of uses — as a hedge or edging, mingled with other shrubs, or massed together for a stunning display. The main attraction of potentilla is its long flowering period, from June until frost, with flowers of white, creamy white to bright yellow, or rosy pink.

- Serviceberries are wonderfully useful garden shrubs, with the smallest species — the Saskatoonberry — hardy on the prairies, where its cultivars are grown as a commercial fruit crop.

- Lilacs are tried and true garden favourites. Common lilac and French hybrids like 'Madame Lemoine' or 'Sensation' can be used as very tall background shrubs in a mixed border or with other shrubs as a screen. In a very small garden, however, a better choice might be a smaller lilac such as Persian lilac, littleleaf lilac, Meyer lilac, or Korean lilac.

- Deutzia has clouds of smallish white flowers and, like spiraea, is useful where a low-maintenance shrub is needed. It leafs out quite late, however, so its early twigginess may not be to everyone's taste.

- Weigelas are sturdy, dependable shrubs that fill design holes in a spring garden and bloom reliably in various shades of pink and red.

Dwarf Japanese yew lends itself to clipping for formal designs such as this boxwood parterre.

- Spiraeas, both the spring and summer types, are highly useful in garden design. Among the first to bloom is garland spiraea, its dense, arching branches covered in tiny white flowers. Next comes tall Vanhoutte, or bridalwreath spiraea, very popular as an informal, fountain-shaped hedge and a good choice as a background shrub. All the spiraeas are useful shrubs for a slope, where they help to prevent erosion. In summer, the smaller Bumalda spiraeas begin to flower, many with spectacular foliage. 'Goldflame,' for instance, has new spring growth that's bright bronze-orange, later turning lime-green as the pink flowers emerge, finally turning a beautiful red in autumn. Although the foliage of 'Anthony Waterer' doesn't colour, its bright pink flowers make it a good "filler" shrub in a flower border.

- Hydrangeas offer superb versatility as summer shrubs and grow well in lightly shaded areas. 'Peegee' hydrangea, with its conical, creamy-white blossoms, tends to steal the show and is best used on its own or, if a grafted standard, as a small garden tree.

- Large-flowered rhododendrons and deciduous azaleas look beautiful in a woodland setting where they get morning sun, and afternoon shade. Hardy small-flowered rhododendrons take much more sun. The new 'Northern Lights' series of azaleas are hardy to Zone 4b and produce masses of flowers in late May and early June.

DESIGN TIPS

- Capitalize on your neighbours' assets! You can make your garden appear wider or deeper by matching your neighbour' plantings along your shared property line. For example, if your neighbour has a cedar hedge or row of shrubs such as lilacs at the property line, plant cedars or lilacs next to them on your side of the line. The demarcation between the two properties is softened and both of you will benefit from having a stronger background for your shorter plantings.

- Steal a canopy. Instead of supplying your own canopy, use your neighbour's taller plantings as your canopy. On your side of the line, plant something shorter, then add successively shorter plants in front to taper down to a level suitable to your surroundings. The neighbours' trees add shade, privacy, and protection to your surroundings, too.

STANDARDS

S ome people call them "a shrub on a stick" — it's a good way of remembering what they look like. Look for low standard evergreens in topiary shapes, weeping mulberries, euonymus, viburnums, caraganas, and flowering almonds. They're great because they don't take up a lot of space and you can maximize your planting area by planting under them. Plant them in containers to flank a door for a formal and attractive entry to the house.

D E S I G N   T I P S

- Don't forget to start with the big elements of your planting plan — it's what the pros do. Use large shrubs to frame a view or hide unattractive views. Once they're in place, plant the middle range of plants, finishing with annuals, perennials, vines, and groundcovers. This terracing or tapering produces a lush, integrated look.

- Start with a tree such as flowering crab, which has a single trunk, in contrast to the tall multi-stemmed shrubs you add next — forsythia, weigela, purple leaf sandcherry, lilac, mock orange, or honeysuckle. To avoid a rigid, static look to your planting, arrange the shrubs in loose "triangle groups." Plant a bush at each point of an imaginary triangle. Keep the triangle a bit off-centre for a more natural look.

- Add some mid-range shrubs between the larger plants — spiraea, potentilla, hydrangea, azalea, or hardy shrub roses.

- Use vines on a fence or to cover a wall.

- Place some easy-care groundcovers such as cotoneaster or euonymus.

- Finally, fill in the holes with tall perennials such as daylilies, monkshood, astilbe, or delphinium. Weave the plantings among the shrubs so that as the perennials grow, they will peek out enticingly from among the green of the shrubbery and groundcovers.

A cluster of pots soften the corner of this stone house, adding a pleasing splash of colour. The standard (or tree-form) pink hibiscus will flower all summer long if regularly fertilized.

YEAR-ROUND BEAUTY

Most Canadians can't garden for 12 months of the year — our climate just won't allow it. But that doesn't mean you can't have something attractive to look at even in the depths of winter and you can do it using only trees and shrubs! We've got some ideas for the months that are most likely to present a problem — spring, fall and winter. By picking and choosing from the plants in each season, you can have something of interest in your garden throughout the year.

DESIGNING FOR FRAGRANCE

One of the truly romantic aspects of design is the use of perfumed shrubs and flowers to create a fragrant garden. How? By placing scented plants like the trumpet lily 'Anaconda' adjacent to a deck or patio, under a window, beside a front door, along a path, or merely close to a spot where you can relax and inhale deeply! Choose plants that are late-spring or summer bloomers, since that's when you'll be outdoors.

White-flowered plants are highly visible in the garden after dark and some, like fragrant white nicotiana, datura, and annual evening stock, emit their perfume only at night.

Try the following perfumed plants in your late spring or summer garden: selected lilacs; clove currant; daphnes; Koreanspice viburnum; 'Burkwood' viburnum; fragrant snowball viburnum; selected roses (especially old roses); summer-sweet; 'Goldflame' honeysuckle; mock orange; regal, trumpet, and Oriental lily hybrids; pinks and carnations; flowering tobacco; and evening stock.

Deutzia is a versatile low shrub for spring, when
it blooms at the same time as common lilac.

TEXTURE AND COLOUR

An important element of putting plants together in a pleasing way is the texture created by the leaves, bark, and flowers. Bark can be shiny, smooth, wrinkled, or shredded. Leaves are glossy, dull, incised, solid. Use different textures to achieve contrast or similar textures to produce harmony.

Colour comes from leaves as well as flowers. Choose shrubs, perennials, and annuals that have silver, gold, or burgundy incised, or solid foliage to add variety and subtle tones to your "palette".

TREES AND SHRUBS FOR SPRING

I n the spring garden, flowering trees and shrubs can complement colourful tulips and daffodils or claim the glory all for themselves.

Flowering crabapples are glorious symbols of spring, and their berries can be highly decorative in summer, fall and winter.

- Crabapples offer many design possibilities. The narrow-growing and extremely hardy Siberian crabapple is good for tight spaces. The small Sargent's crab is ideal as a specimen for a small patio. Both have white flowers and small red fruit.

- Serviceberries are three-season plants: early white blossoms, edible summer berries, and foliage that turns a stunning red in autumn. Grow downy, Allegheny, and apple serviceberry as small trees or large shrubs.

- Magnolias, either the large saucer or tulip magnolia or the smaller shrubby star magnolia and its many fine cultivars, are great favourites for spring but they're not hardy across the country. Don't plant them in a low-lying area where late frost can damage the emerging flowers. Although the saucer magnolia needs a spacious planting site to handle its mature size, star magnolia is a good choice for a small garden.

- Japanese gardens are enhanced by flowering Japanese cherries, and even the tiniest patio or large balcony planter can feature a tree-form flowering almond.

- Japanese tree lilac, with its long, creamy flower panicles, is a low-care choice for a mixed border, especially when underplanted with late spring perennials like peonies and catmint.

- The fabulous green and white leaves of dogwood brighten up a dark corner — it tolerates shade, making it really versatile. Kousa flowering dogwood has lovely white flower bracts in late June and is hardier than native flowering dogwood. Pagoda or alternate-leafed dogwood is a very adaptable native shrub that fits well into a naturalistic garden and is striking, even in winter, with its tiered branches.

IMPORTANCE OF TREES IN GARDEN DESIGN

- Provide focus and sense of permanence
- Add a vertical dimension
- Block or screen a view
- Frame a vista
- Provide privacy
- Create a windbreak when planted *en masse*
- Provide shade and coolness

TREES AND SHRUBS FOR AUTUMN

Not all of us are summer gardeners. Some people spend a great deal of the summer away; these are the gardeners who revel in the autumn garden. They paint their garden canvas with the ephemeral but spectacularly beautiful seasonal hues of trees and shrubs. The planting and design basics — the sequence of planting, terracing the layers — are applied in the fall garden with special emphasis on colour and structure.

In the early fall, garden tones change to bright oranges, reds, and yellows. As leaves start to fall, the underlying structure of trees and shrubs is revealed. Evergreens take on importance in the fall garden. If they've been anchoring the back of a border or bed, they come into prominence as the small trees, shrubs, and perennials around them begin to decline.

- Dwarf burning bush is one of the easiest-care shrubs to give form (if not flowers) to a sunny shrub border. But in October, when its leaves turn a fluorescent, rich pink, and in winter, when its corky winged branches stand out in the snowy landscape, burning bush demonstrates its worth.

- Other fine fall-colouring shrubs include witch hazels, serviceberries, Peking cotoneaster, smoke bush, fothergilla, Amur maple, sumacs, and selected spireas and dogwoods. Even shrubs that have finished flowering have something to offer — the brown dried flower heads of hydrangea complement the fall colours.

- Trees are the quintessential fall-colour plants. Red maple and sugar maple are flamboyant with their familiar yellow, red, and orange foliage. Lacy Japanese maple, can be counted on for a beautiful show. Birches and honey locusts turn yellow, beeches a rich copper, and katsura and ginkgo trees become pyramids of butter yellow.

The ornamental grass Miscanthus 'Purpurascens', turns rich orange-gold in fall, contrasting nicely with the Japanese maple behind it. Right, By using trees and shrubs whose leaves turn colour in fall, you can add interest in your garden for many weeks after the summer show declines.

PERENNIALS AND ANNUALS FOR FALL

Although it's possible to have a spectacular autumn garden composed of trees and shrubs, particular perennials and annuals add their own dash of colour. For rich bright colour in the flowerbed, plant fall monkshoods, chrysanthemums, plumey grasses that add movement as well as colour, asters, boltonia, sweet autumn clematis, and annual flowering kale. Set against a background of berried bushes and the hips of shrub roses, you'll have a stunning fall display.

TREES AND SHRUBS FOR WINTER

When the last autumn leaf is gone and the first dusting of snow appears, evergreens come to the fore. A well-designed garden includes a variety of beautifully shaped and subtly coloured evergreens. But winter interest isn't confined only to evergreens. Many shrubs brighten a wintry scene, even when there's no snow, with textured bark or colourful stems and berries, which provide food for birds.

- To make the most of a blanket of snow, use graceful conifers with lacy branches like weeping hemlock, weeping Norway spruce, or weeping false cypress.

- The colour of some evergreens deepens in winter. 'Rheingold' cedar becomes copper and 'Bar Harbour' juniper turns a soft plum. Other small evergreens take on new prominence as surrounding perennials die back, annuals succumb to frost, and deciduous trees and shrubs lose their leaves. There are many forms to choose from, including the compact, pyramidal shape of dwarf Alberta spruce. Other interesting forms that become more obvious in the winter are standards and topiary shapes, such as pompoms and spirals.

- Put evergreen euonymus and boxwood (formally clipped or allowed to grow naturally) in a part of the garden where winter sun won't scorch their foliage. With small-flowered rhododendrons like 'PJM', whose leaves turn burgundy in winter, they create a lovely year-round texture.

- Many shrubs have colourful stems in winter, particularly the new growth. Two that look beautiful in a spot where sunshine hits them are silverleaf dogwood and its gold-stemmed cousin 'Flaviramea'.

- Winterberry, a deciduous and hardy cousin of holly, likes full sun. The cultivar 'Sparkleberry' has masses of red winter berries.

- Washington thorn is a four-season beauty with creamy flowers on thorny branches in summer, glossy leaves that turn red and orange in fall, and dangling clusters of little red berries that persist all winter.

- Cotoneasters have dense, arching branches and small, jewel-like fruits that last all winter long. Prostrate varieties make excellent drought-tolerant groundcovers.

With a fresh blanket of snow, evergreens and seasonal container arrangements heighten interest in the winter garden.

PLANTING TIPS

- If a plant will grow in Zone 2, it will grow in warmer zones, as well.

- Some plants survive better in colder zones if there's a good covering of snow — the snow acts as insulation. In warmer zones, such as 6 and 7, the snow cover is not always consistent in the winter and can expose plants to harsh winds, strong sun, and fluctuating temperatures.

GOOD BETS FOR HEDGING

A hedge is a living fence. Like a fence, it is used to define the boundaries of your property, separate areas within a garden, delineate garden rooms, establish a front-yard courtyard, provide privacy, buffer street noise, or define the kids' play area.

- For an informal hedge, find a shrub that fits the space so you won't need to be constantly pruning. Good choices include hardy shrub roses like the red Explorer 'Champlain'. Bridalwreath spiraea makes a fountain-shaped hedge and has pleasing autumn colour too; smaller spiraeas are good hedging plants within the garden. The dwarf Meyer lilac 'Palibin' makes a beautiful mid-sized hedge and is covered with sweet-scented, mauve flower panicles in late spring.

- Deciduous hedges that create box-shaped privacy walls generally require at least one annual clipping. Old-fashioned stalwarts like Amur privet are still popular, but can become leggy without constant shearing. Where hardiness is an issue, try common ninebark or caragana for a tall hedge; Alpine currant or blue Arctic willow for a lower one.

- Of the needled evergreens, white cedar (or arborvitae) and yew make the best hedging materials. Cedar grows very tall, making it a good "leafy wall," but to keep it dense at the bottom, it needs regular shearing. (See *Care* for tips on pruning an evergreen hedge.) Dense yew and Hick's yew are slower-growing but tolerate deep shade. They are good choices where a low, evergreen hedge is desired.

- Broadleafed evergreen hedges such as the euonymus 'Emerald Gaiety' or 'Sarcoxie' make wonderful hedging and are alternatives to boxwood. They can be tightly clipped for formal designs, or they can be allowed to adopt a softer, more natural shape. Green cultivars of euonymus should be grown in shade or in morning sun since late-day winter sun can burn the foliage, creating an eyesore until new foliage leafs out in spring.

ROOFTOP HEDGE

Just because you garden off the ground doesn't mean you can't have a hedge. It provides privacy just as it does on the ground.

- An excellent choice for a container hedge is privet. It's tough and withstands wind and cold.

- Alpine currant is ideal for a low container hedge in sun or shade.

A low hedge can be used to separate planting beds from a patio or lawn.

WOODY VINES

Sooner or later, most gardeners turn to house and garage walls, fences, trellises, gates, pergolas, and host shrubs and trees that allow them to take their love of gardening in a new direction: upward.

Vines fit the bill. Vines are one of the most versatile categories of plants — they provide a great variety of colour, texture, growth habit, and flowering sequence.

Some vines need something to twist around — a man-made structure or a tree or shrub to scramble through. Other vines need a surface to cling to, such as a wall or fence. Knowing how your vines climb will mean you can provide the correct support for these wonderful plants.

PERGOLAS AND ARCHES

Sturdy wooden or metal pergolas and arches make excellent focal points in a garden, especially when smothered in a beautiful vine. A rustic arch wreathed in orange-berried bittersweet can offer a pleasant transition from one area to the next. An arbour covered in perfumed honeysuckle or rambling roses is a cozy spot for sitting and reflecting. Big twining vines like kiwi, grape, silverlace, and akebia need sturdy posts, beams and wires — not a flimsy trellis — as their wood ages and their long branches extend from the trunk. An elderly orange trumpet creeper can grow heavy enough to topple a fence, so give it the support it needs from the start or plan on annual pruning.

WALLS

Foliage vines like Boston ivy, Virginia creeper, English ivy, and the occasional flowering vine such as climbing hydrangea, scale vertical surfaces by means of aerial rootlets or sucker pads — little stickers that adhere with a vengeance to mortar, brick, and wood.

TIPS

- Dress up a brick wall with an ornament or decorative plaque, a pot or piece of iron grill work, then train the vine around it, clipping stray stems and leaves to display the ornamental addition.

- A vigorous vine, such as silverlace vine, will quickly cover what most people consider an eyesore — a chain link fence.

- Other good vines for chain link fences include 'Goldflame' honeysuckle, akebia (also called chocolate vine), and clematis.

Decorative trellis dresses up an otherwise barren wall which can then be softened with lush climbing vines.

CLEMATIS, THE SOCIAL CLIMBER

There's nothing quite like a clematis vine in full, spectacular bloom to fill you with joy and make you feel satisfied with your gardening skills. With masses of velvety flowers in rich purple, wine, red, pink, mauve, lavender, blue, white, and even yellow, there's a clematis that's perfect for every garden and every gardening season.

There's also nothing quite like a clematis to challenge the conventional way we grow our vines. While you might instinctively think "trellis" as you ponder where to plant your new clematis, consider some other creative approaches to using it in your design. One is to plant two different coloured clematis cultivars — popular purple 'Jackmanii' and pink 'Comtesse de Bouchaud' make lovely companions — on either side of a rose arch that leads from one garden area to another. It's preferable that both clematis are Group 3 (summer hybrids) so they bloom at the same time and can be cut back hard in spring when you tend to any required rose pruning.

RAYMOND EVISON

When we think "clematis," we think "Raymond Evison." He's been growing and breeding clematis for more than 35 years at his nursery in Guernsey in the Channel Islands. He goes beyond growing and breeding, though — he writes about clematis and searches the world over for new species. When we wanted to introduce clematis suitable to the Canadian climate, there was only one person to talk to. Raymond has assisted us in putting together our collection of clematis for our Canadian conditions. He ships the young stock to our grower, who plants them and nurtures them through our long winter so we know they're hardy when our customers buy them.

Clematis 'Beth Currie' is a large-flowered Group 2 hybrid ideally suited for container growing and newly-introduced by Raymond Evison.

THE VERSATILE CLEMATIS

Roses and clematis make lovely partners, but don't stop there. Clematis likes to wind itself around obelisks and trellises and to make its way through shrubs and trees. You can also use it as a groundcover.

- Spring-blooming *Clematis alpina* and *Clematis macropetala* can be allowed to scramble in a rock garden with alpine plants that flower at the same time. When these Group 1 clematis stop blooming, cut them back so they have the rest of the summer to make new compact growth, on which next year's flowers will appear.

- Whether you grow your clematis against a trellis, a post, a fence or wall, give some thought to the colour effect you want to achieve. Purple or white flowers look better than reddish-pink tones on orange brick; white and pale colours stand out on green foliage; lavender and pink flowers are beautiful on gray-stained wood.

- Let a herbaceous clematis like August-blooming *C. heracleifolia* scramble through the perennial border or encourage a white September-blooming cloud of small-flowered sweet autumn clematis, *C. terniflora*, to fling itself over the top of a tall, wooden pergola.

OUR FAVOURITE COMBOS

Here are some of our favourite clematis combinations. To create your own, research the pruning group your choices belong to. First, match plants by their pruning group — a group 2 clematis goes with another group 2. Within the group, choose pairs or groups of three, looking for colours that complement one another. Here are some to try.

'Anna Louise' with 'Ramona' or 'Snow Queen'
'Nelly Moser' with 'Ramona' or 'William Kennet'
'Pink Champagne' with 'Violet Charm' or 'Masquerade'

Some threesomes we like:

'Carnaby' with 'Dr. Ruppel' and 'Edouard Desfosse'
'Ascotiensis' with 'Ville de Lyon' and 'Ernest Markham'

The lavender-purple clematis 'General Sikorski' looks particularly attractive arrayed against a gray-stained trellis.

JOIN THE GROUP

By selecting clematis from all three pruning groups, you can have vines in bloom from spring through fall, in an incredible variety of colours, with flowers that range from small, nodding bells to huge, flat doubles.

PRUNING GROUP 1

- Clematis in this group bloom in the spring and have small flowers. They bloom on shoots produced in the previous season, so prune them after they've finished flowering but no later than the end of June or the new growth will not ripen sufficiently to produce flower buds for next year's growth. However, annual pruning is not necessary except to keep them under control.

- They're ideal for growing through evergreen or deciduous trees, on walls or fences, or through other wall-trained shrubs.

- Names to look for: *Clematis alpina* 'Pink Flamingo' (any clematis with montana, alpina or macropetala in its botanical name is from Group 1).

PRUNING GROUP 2

- This group flowers in early summer, producing large double or single blooms. They flower on the previous season's growth and should be pruned hard the first spring after planting. Thereafter, cut out dead wood and weak growth in early spring and prune the remaining stems to the strongest leaf buds, 30 to 150 cm (1 to 5 feet) above the ground. Group 2 clematis often produce flowers on their new growth in late summer or fall.

- Grow these clematis through deciduous or evergreen trees or shrubs, as well as over fences or through trellises.

- Names to look for: 'Anna Louise', 'Bee's Jubilee', 'Edouard Desfosse', 'Scartho Gem,' 'Nelly Moser', 'Henryi'

PRUNING GROUP 3

- These summer-flowering clematis bloom on the current season's growth often producing blooms from June to October. To ensure blooms spread evenly over the growth, and not just at the top of old stems, prune hard to a pair of healthy fat buds within 30 cm (1 foot) above the ground.

- Grow through sturdy deciduous or evergreen shrubs or an obelisk. Remove the old growth in late fall and you can appreciate the form of the obelisk during the winter. Plant low shrubs around the obelisk to protect the plant's roots.

- Names to look for: 'Ville de Lyon', 'Polish Spirit', 'Petit Faucon', 'Ascotiensis'

LATE SUMMER AND FALL FLOWERING CLEMATIS

These Group 3 plants flower in late summer and fall, make good groundcovers, and can be trained through small deciduous trees or shrubs. Because they are pruned back hard in spring, the pruning needs of the host plant can be tended to at the same time. Ensure that the clematis is planted at least 30 cm (1 foot) from the tree trunk or shrub base so the vine receives enough water and does not suffer root competition from the host. Select a flower colour that complements the colour of the foliage or host tree.

- to grow through small trees or as groundcovers, try 'Madame Julia Correvon', or 'Venosa Violacea'
- for growing through small trees, look for 'Polish Spirit'

TIPS

- Clematis like their roots shaded. The shade can be provided by other plants (the shady side of tree is great), a garden ornament or statue, a lovely rock, a bench or other piece of furniture. Use an existing garden structure to provide the needed protection — the shade cast by the corner of a deck or step, for example.

- Plant your new clematis about 6 cm (2 1/2 inches) deeper than it was in the pot — when clematis is planted this way, it's less likely to be killed by wilt, a fungal disease. Although wilt may affect the top of these plants, the roots will be healthy enough to send up strong new shoots.

- Remember when gardening books told you clematis needed limey (alkaline) soil? It's a myth! It's true that one particular type of clematis — old man's beard — loves lime and in the past, new varieties were grafted on to this species. But today's varieties are happy in any soil, as long as it's rich and well-drained, amended with plenty of well-rotted manure.

- If you're attaching a trellis to a wall for a clematis — or any other twining climber — don't attach the trellis flush to the wall. Leave some space between the trellis and the wall so the clematis can get around the slats of the trellis.

- When you plant a wall-trained clematis, be sure to dig the hole at least 30 cm (1 foot) from the wall to ensure that the plant receives adequate rainfall.

- Extend the "flowering season" of such favourites as lilac, magnolia, and flowering crab by planting a clematis at their base. The host plant becomes a living trellis. It's best to use a Group 3 cultivar that gets cut back hard in spring; this will allow you to deal with the pruning requirements of the host shrub at the same time.

ROMANCING THE ROSE

I f you love roses the way we do, we don't have to describe the plea-
sure you feel as you watch that slender bud open. But there's
more to them than their gorgeous blooms. Whether you devote an
entire bed to roses — the best way to grow hybrid teas, flori-
bunds, and grandifloras — or nestle them among other
shrubs and perennials, there's a wonderful array of choice. The
common requirement for roses is sun, but from there you can find a rose to
fill nearly any need. Choose from an amazing selection of colours; double
or single flowers; bushes that produce hips and those that don't; minia-
tures, mid-size, and far-reaching climbers and ramblers; strongly or mildly
scented; high maintenance or easy care — you make the choice!

HYBRID TEAS, FLORIBUNDAS, AND GRANDIFLORAS

Hybrid teas ('Peace', 'First Prize', and 'Vienna Charm' are examples)
are the prima donnas of the rose world. Their large, sensuous flowers,
borne singly on long stems, are often fragrant and excellent for cutting.
Floribundas like 'Hans Christian Anderson' and 'Iceberg' and grandifloras
like 'Queen Elizabeth' are shrubby roses that bear their clustered blooms
non-stop from late June into fall.

This group of roses is more demanding than shrub roses. Our advice to
gardeners who can't bear the thought of doing without these beauties but
who have limited maintenance time is to devote a single bed to them. They
all need the same conditions: sun, well-drained soil, winter protection, and
pruning. In addition, they are prone to the same problems, mainly black
spot and powdery mildew. It's more efficient and kinder to the environment
to be able to apply chemical treatments, if you decide to use them, in one
spot in the garden, where they are directed only at the plants that need
them. By grouping these roses, you will also improve the air circulation
around them, thereby reducing the possibility of disease.

The ultra-hardy Explorer rose 'William Baffin'
has thick, abundant canes and is excellent as a
tall, arching shrub or vigorous, large climber.

MODERN REPEAT-BLOOMING SHRUB ROSES

Shrub roses are the easiest and most satisfying roses to incorporate into the garden. The flowering types include singles, doubles, and clusters, and the flowering periods are long.

Study their characteristics to see how to use them in a shrub bed or perennial border. They can provide contrast in texture, height, and colour, or act as complements to shrubs and flowers of similar habit. When positioning them, follow the "triangle" formation mentioned earlier and create a hierarchy of heights.

Not only do modern shrub roses have an important place among other flowers and shrubs, but their care demands are minimal. Like all roses, most of them need sun, but they need little pruning — only what is necessary to cut out dead wood, keep rampant growth under control, or to tidy up the shape.

David Austin roses combine the best of the old roses — scent and lush flowers — with the best of new roses — repeat flowering and easy care. Rose breeder David Austin bred and re-bred exquisitely beautiful, perfumed "old" roses like the Gallicas, Centifolias, and Damasks, which flower only once in early summer, with repeat-flowering floribundas and hybrid teas. The results included sensational roses like tall yellow 'Graham Thomas', pink 'Mary Rose', red 'L.D. Braithwaite' and shell-pink 'Heritage'. 'Charles Austin' is a tall apricot beauty that looks sensational with blue delphiniums.

CANADIAN ROSES

Canadian-bred shrub roses are among the hardiest in the world — and the most beautiful. From Agriculture Canada's research station in Morden, Manitoba, came the Morden series roses, including red-and-pink striped 'Morden Ruby', tall 'Morden Centennial' with its hybrid-tea-like blooms and deep-pink 'Morden Amorette'.

The Ottawa-bred "Explorer" series gave us low, mid-sized and tall shrub roses with names borrowed from early explorers in Canadian history. Low shrubs like 'Henry Hudson' make good dense groundcovers or low hedges. Mid-sized shrubs that can substitute for less-hardy floribundas include pink 'John Davis', carmine-pink 'John Franklin', and red 'Champlain'. Taller shrubs for mixed borders include red 'Alexander Mackenzie' and pale-pink 'Martin Frobisher'. Two extremely tall Explorer roses that can be used as hardy climbers include black-spot resistant 'William Baffin' and 'John Cabot', which is also good as a tall arching shrub in a mixed shrub border.

A ROSE FOR EVERY GARDEN

Roses best suited for natural or low-maintenance gardens are those developed from crosses with the rugged and extremely hardy *Rosa rugosa*. Rugosa hybrids tend to have a spicy perfume and are very disease-resistant, with their main flush of flowers in early summer. Excellent choices include crimson-purple 'Hansa', lilac-pink 'Therese Bugnet' and strong-scented 'Roseraie de l'Hay'.

Climbing roses look enchanting gracing an arch, pergola, or house or garage wall. A few distinguish themselves by performing superbly year after year. One is the crimson-and-white single-flowered 'Dortmund'.

Low shrub roses can be grown as a hedge or allowed to clamber through an airy fence.

Among the best shrub roses for groundcover use or for mass planting are diminutive ones like the pink polyantha rose 'The Fairy' and creamy-white 'Sea Foam'. Excellent taller shrubs include the aptly named 'Carefree Wonder'. French-bred Meidiland roses like 'Bonica' also perform admirably with a minimum of fuss.

LAYERING PERENNIALS FOR MAXIMUM EFFECT

When you're planning where the tall back-of-border perennials will go, arrange them so they weave in and out with plants of other heights. The effect can be a lively punctuation or a gradual undulation of height, depending on how you partner your tall plants.

Spiky delphinium and monkshood are tall plants in shades of blue; fluffy filipendula and rounded Joe pye weed have warmer pink colours. The daisy-like flowers of the grey-headed coneflower add a bright spot of yellow around their grey cone. Use white candelabra-like snakeroot, feathery goatsbeard, or rounded boltonia to act as transitions from one group of colours to another or to soften and cool an otherwise hot combination.

For the front of a perennial border, use short, mounding plants that create a graceful transition to the lawn, sidewalk or patio. Consider perennial geraniums, lambs' ears, hostas, sedums, coral bells and dwarf asters.

Perennials don't need to be confined to a border — they can stand on their own, too. A bright patch of ground phlox by a front door looks wonderful in the spring when it's covered in masses of flowers, and its spiky green foliage looks attractive during the rest of the year. Masses of daylilies make a stunning sight in flower; before and after flowering, their graceful slender leaves make a lovely textural contrast to a neat well-kept lawn or complement the oval leaves of lower-growing hostas.

SHAPE

Plants can be upright, flat-topped, arching, rounded, sprawling or spreading. Combine various shapes, such as a narrowly upright or spiky plant like great blue lobelia to contrast a rounded form like summer phlox. Or use spherical shapes like spiky globe thistle or fuzzy alliums to add interest.

Daisies, which are tall and profuse, give height and fill in around skimpier plants. The flowerheads of these plants provide contrasting shapes too.

Astilbes and hostas create a pleasant contrast of form and are useful perennials for a shady garden.

A Perennial Starter Kit

If you're new to gardening, here's a sunny border "starter kit": 10 hard-working plants for flowers and foliage from early spring to fall.

1. **Perennial Candytuft:** Good front-of-border or rockery plant with masses of snowy white flowers in spring. Evergreen; shear after flowering ends. Good with late tulips; blooms in April.

2. **Coralbells:** Worthy of inclusion in any garden because of their beautiful, marbled leaves and slender stems hung with panicles of small red, coral, pink or white blossoms. Very long-flowering, from June to August.

3. **Peony:** Whether single or double, white, pink, red, coral or yellow — there's a peony for every garden. Long-lived and undemanding, peonies pair well with other June flowers, including irises and poppies.

4. **Threadleaf Coreopsis:** Good front-of-border plant with masses of small, yellow daisies and finely cut foliage. 'Zagreb' is knee-high with gold flowers; 'Moonbeam' is shorter with pale-yellow flowers; flowers all summer.

5. **Catmint:** Choose either dwarf catmint for sprawling at the front of the border or tall Siberian catmint for a good "blue" touch in June. Shear dwarf catmint back after flowering for repeat bloom.

6. **Daylily:** Thousands of cultivars from dwarf to tall, for sun or shade, in every colour of the rainbow, with flowering times from late spring to fall. A good repeat-bloomer is dwarf 'Stella d'Oro' with gold-yellow flowers.

7. **Summer Phlox:** Old-fashioned mid-border perennial with large flower-heads in white, pink and red. Needs moist soil.

8. **Purple Coneflower:** Easy-care full-sun native for mid-late summer. Red-violet to rose-pink daisy-like flowers attract butterflies.

9. **Rudbeckia 'Goldsturm':** Another low-maintenance native daisy; a good, long-blooming (from mid to late summer) cousin of wild blackeyed susan.

10. **Showy Stonecrop:** Late-flowering sedums like 'Brilliant' and 'Autumn Joy' are drought-tolerant, long-blooming and combine nicely with mums.

Purple coneflower and rudbeckia 'Goldsturm' bloom over a long period in late summer and are wonderful for attracting butterflies.

The plants in the Starter Kit are all hardy — that means they'll all survive in Zone 3, and many are hardy even in Zone 2. Where you live will have an effect on the plants you can grow (see *Care* for more information on zones). For example, Zone 2 is farther north than Zone 5, and if you live there, you'll have fewer plants from which to choose. Adventuresome gardeners, though, learn tricks to increase the range of more tender plants they can grow by creating sheltered spots that will trap warmth and by applying a winter mulch over plants of borderline hardiness.

GREAT GROUNDCOVERS

Groundcover plants are sometimes used as an alternative to a lawn, but there are lots of other great uses for them.

- Plant them at the base of a specimen tree to highlight it.

- Use them where it's hard to grow anything else — plants with variegated leaves can brighten the area under a big shade tree.

- Use groundcovers as lawn replacements in small gardens where it's tricky to manoeuvre a lawn mower.

- Plant them inside low boxwood hedges to make an attractive and formal knot garden.

- Put them between stepping stones to fill in bare spots and discourage weeds.

- Grow them in those forgotten areas — by the garage, down the side of the house.

- Plant a groundcover or larger plant, such as a sumac, on a difficult-to-mow slope, to make mowing unnecessary and help stop soil erosion.

- Make a tapestry of colours with sedums and low-growing non-flowering plants. The subtle combination of colours and textures of sedums can be a real knock-out in a small garden.

Now that you can see the varied ways to use groundcovers, let's look at some low growers. We're using a fairly narrow definition here — a plant that doesn't grow much over 30 cm (12 inches). Many other plants that grow taller can be considered groundcovers for their vigorous growth and ability to cover a wide area.

- Groundcover perennials include epimedium; ornamental strawberry 'Pink Panda'; sweet woodruff; lamium; blue vinca or periwinkle; gold-leafed creeping Jenny; pachysandra; creeping sedums; thymes; prostrate veronicas; English ivy; lily-of-the-valley; native and European gingers; violets. Don't forget clematis and other vines make valuable groundcovers.

- Some very low shrubs that fall within our 30 cm (12-inch) maximum include wintergreen, bunchberry (a member of the dogwood family), cotoneaster, bearberry, and horizontal juniper.

Shade-tolerant groundcovers can be used under trees where lawn is difficult to grow.

ADDING THE ANNUALS

While shrubs and trees give the garden canvas its strong lines, foliage its green wash, and perennial flowers its blocks of seasonal colour, annuals are the highlights of brilliance that tie the scene together.

COUNT THE WAYS

Annuals offer tremendous scope for different uses . . .

- They're versatile, with something for every type of garden, from delicate flowers to creeping plants that soften the edges of containers to tall accents to fabulous foliage. Use them to match the theme of the garden or provide contrast.

- You can change the look of the garden every year. One year it can be quite formal, the next more casual, all with a different choice and placement of annuals.

- You can experiment with colours, figure out what works best and what you like most.

- Although many annuals flower cheerfully all season long, there are others we like for their seasonality: pansies and violas in the spring; cosmos in the middle of summer; cleome in late summer; and flowering kale in the autumn.

- We love to use them in containers — so much so that we've got a whole book devoted to them, *Containers*.

- Annuals can be used to extend the flowering season and fill holes in a perennial garden. Shorter annuals like impatiens, verbena and nasturtium enhance front-of-border perennials while tall annuals such as cosmos and larkspur combine beautifully with late summer perennials like phlox and globe thistle.

- Annuals can be used to enhance a colour-themed garden. For a pink and white vignette, combine pink lavatera and verbena, white nicotiana, and pink cleome.

Most Canadians don't plant out their annuals until late May but we love to put pansies and violas in a pot on the front step even when a few flakes of snow are falling. These hardy little annuals can withstand some frost, so when your garden centre puts them out for sale, load up with them!

Sometimes they're the only splash of colour around while you wait for the bulbs to put on their show. When the hot weather arrives and they lose their energy, replace them with more seasonal flowers.

Mandevilla 'Summer Snow' clambers up and through a bamboo stake tripod in a large decorative planter.

ANNUAL VINES

For a quick cover-up or to add vertical interest on a deck or balcony garden, look to annual vines.

• Plant morning glories and moonflower together to climb over a fence or up a trellis or obelisk. You'll have heavenly white evening blooms from the moonflower and red, white, purple, or blue flowers during the day from the morning glory. Or let a morning glory scramble through a sweet autumn clematis for a lovely sight in late summer.

• Potato vine blooms from the middle of summer until frost hits. The flowers are small, white or blue-white stars. It can grow to 6 m (20 feet) in a season, but don't be afraid to cut it back to control its growth. On the other hand, if you're interested in covering up an unsightly view, let it go!

• Old-fashioned favourites are sweet peas. In a container or set in the flowerbed with a bit of support, you'll have pretty blooms that make good cut flowers for a cottagey bouquet — and the more you cut, the more they'll produce.

• Looking for the exotic? Try passion flower. It's a fast grower in the sun and produces amazing intricate purple, blue, red, or white flowers. It's fragrant and blooms all summer, providing quick shade if grown over an arbour.

• Mandevilla is a tender vine native to the tropics but increasingly popular in our summer gardens for its lush, shiny foliage and abundant pink or white blossoms. It prefers very warm temperatures but is easy-to-grow and can reach more than 5 metres (15 feet).

CHOICE ANNUALS . . .

FOR THE SHADE

- Impatiens, famous for its amazing flower production in the shade and its great fluorescent colours, makes wonderful billowy mounds under trees, as edging for shady borders, or in containers set in a shaded corner. Impatiens also gives the gardener the opportunity to do some mixing and matching, especially if you get varieties that have multi-coloured blooms.

- Fibrous begonias create a consistent, dainty, and neat hedge. Choose all the same colour or mix some white plants with a few delicate pinks for a pretty combination.

- Coleus is valuable for its foliage and the colour contrast it provides — set off some pink or white impatiens with a variety of coleus sporting burgundy leaves.

FOR THE SUN

- 'Blue Horizon' ageratum not only has a marvellous blue colour, it grows to an impressive 45 cm (1 1/2 feet). Partner it with a tall white marigold or snapdragon for a smashing contrast of colour and form.

- 'Floralace' dianthus is a great improvement over other dianthus. Not only has this one got the largest flowers of any dianthus, it blooms much longer than any others. It stands up to the heat, so you can use it with other similar plants.

- A tall and graceful plant, the cheerful cosmos can't be beat. Its ferny foliage adds lightness to a composition, whether it's in the garden or a bouquet of cut flowers. In a gentle breeze, a swaying cosmos gives life and movement.

- In a rock garden, on a sunny slope, in cracks in pavement or tucked between patio stones, portulaca is a star. Its deceptively fragile-looking flowers open wide in the sun and its spiky foliage withstands baking heat.

Low annuals like blue salvia 'Victoria', impatiens, verbena and silvery-gray licorice plant lend themselves to a layered arrangement at the front of a border.

MAKE ROOM IN YOUR GARDEN

Some of the great new annuals we've seen include 'Blue Horizon' ageratum; solid-colour portulaca in mouth-watering soft colours; the 'Purple Wave' and 'Pink Wave' petunias, which produce a carpet of flowers; 'Fiesta Double' petunia, a sweet compact dwarf that won't get leggy; 'Quartz' scarlet verbenas with masses of brilliant red blooms; dahliettas, like small mums in good strong colours; 'Fiesta' double impatiens.

FLOWERS, VEGETABLES AND HERBS

Roses with radishes? Spinach with spiraea? Why not? There's no dictate of design that says vegetables need to be hidden away. On the contrary, if you love growing your own produce, celebrate it by giving it pride of place in your garden!

HERBS

If you love cooking with herbs, it's a good idea to plan for a grouping of attractive pots near the kitchen door so favourites like basil, mint, chives, tarragon, rosemary, oregano, and parsley can be easily harvested. Perennial herbs with a mounding habit such as thyme, sage (including lovely gold-variegated cultivars), and lavender make excellent front-of-border plants. They also look charming when grown with silvery aromatic herbs like artemesia and germander in an Elizabethan-style knot garden.

The brilliant blue, nodding blossoms of annual borage have a cucumber flavor. Apart from looking gorgeous in a flower border, they can be used in vinegars, as a garnish, or dried.

PLANT COMBO

Annual and perennial herbs provide texture and look great planted in a container with flowering plants. The airy, yellow flowers of dill look beautiful paired with bright summer flowers like gaillardia. Dill also combines nicely with bronze-red perennial helenium and annual pink cosmos.

The airy yellow flowers of dill pair nicely with bronze and orange gloriosa daisies.

HARDY BULBS FOR SPRING

Spending long hours in chilly autumn weather planting bulbs that won't even begin to poke their noses out of the ground for at least six months is proof positive that gardening is as much about hope as it is about gratification. They're the first sign that spring has arrived, and their colours appear extra brilliant against the newly revealed soil.

- Plant daffodils, tulips, hyacinths, and other large bulbs in masses of six or more; small bulbs like crocus, scilla, puschkinia, and grape hyacinth can be planted in drifts of twenty or more. Bulb foliage needs to "ripen" or turn yellow to feed next year's bulb, so plant them among emerging perennials that will hide all those dying leaves.

- Naturalize daffodils, crocuses, blue chionodoxa, and scilla in the lawn or in long grass close to a tree trunk where they can be left unmown until their leaves ripen.

- Design "vignettes" with shrubs, early perennials, and spring bulbs. Underplant serviceberry, forsythia, or star magnolia, for example, with early daffodils, blue chionodoxa, blue pulmonaria, and dusky purple hellebores. Or plant red-and-yellow tulip 'Belcanto' in a frothy yellow carpet of cushion spurge.

- Combine the very late Viridiflora or "green" tulips like 'Spring Green' in a lightly shaded area with ferns and Solomon's seals. Mix the fabulous spring allium 'Purple Sensation' with mauve sweet rocket, pink bleeding hearts, and a late tulip like 'Rosy Wings'. Or brighten up a sea of blue catmint or forget-me-not with orange tulips and spiky blue camassia.

- Combine blue grape hyacinths in a rock garden, with a small, red Kaufmanniana tulip like 'Stresa' or a tiny, mid-season narcissus like 'Minnow'. And try raspberry-pink aubrieta with grape hyacinths and pink windflowers.

- Use shade-tolerant Spanish bluebells (or wood hyacinths) as a carpet for brilliant orange azaleas. Or pair them with a lovely Japanese tree peony.

- Plant alliums, especially spring-bloomers like 'Purple Sensation' which looks gorgeous with late tulips.

The leaves of tulips and other spring bulbs must be allowed to turn yellow after the flowers fade, in order to photosynthesize fully and nourish next year's developing flower bud.

THE BULBS OF SUMMER

HARDY LILIES

What would our gardens be without lilies? Whether undemanding early-bloomers like the Asiatic hybrids, shade-lovers like June's Martagons, July-flowering trumpets with their intoxicating perfume, or the spicily scented Oriental hybrids of August, lilies are the quintessential summer garden bulb. Plant them in early spring or in autumn at the same time as tulips and daffodils in groups of three to five in the perennial border, pairing them with companion plants that bloom at the same time. Asiatic hybrids, for example, look lovely with delphiniums, coreopsis, veronica, and roses; try the trumpets and Oriental hybrids with blackeyed susans, summer phlox, and purple coneflowers.

TENDER SUMMER BULBS, CORMS, AND TUBERS

Lift these bulbs in fall and store them indoors for winter, or treat them as annuals and purchase anew each spring. Tuberous begonias are extremely useful in a shady garden where their luscious blooms make good companions to ferns; they can be started indoors from tubers, or purchased as pot plants. As for dahlias, the smaller ones are easy to take care of, but the large ones give a dramatic effect with their big dinner-plate heads and long stems. They're great for cutting, too.

As a foliage plant in shade, caladium or elephant ears is invaluable for its big, richly coloured, heart-shaped leaves. Acidanthera has willowy stems topped with elegant, wine-flamed white flowers that perfume an entire garden; plant in drifts over two to three weeks in spring for extended late summer bloom. Canna lilies, which grow 90 to 120 cm (3 to 4 feet), love warm weather and lots of sun. Their "hot" flower colours of orange, yellow, and red lend themselves to designs that pair them with late perennials like rudbeckia 'Herbstonne'. For a softer look, try some of the new coral and pink tones.

Above, *When grown in ideal conditions, most lilies will multiply year after year.* Right, *Hybrid Asiatic lilies are carefree additions to an old-fashioned summer cottage garden.*

MADE IN THE SHADE

With so many excellent plants for the various degrees of garden shade, it's a pity many gardeners give up on a shady garden.

- Shade-tolerant evergreens that can be used to create an overhead canopy and framework include Canada hemlock, yew, green and variegated euonymus, blue holly, and boxwood. Small trees or shrubs for light to moderate shade include serviceberry, snowberry, pagoda and silverleaf dogwood, Japanese maple, privet, honeysuckle, alpine currant, elder, redbud, kerria, nannyberry, rhododendron, and Annabelle hydrangea.

- Bulbs and perennials for shade include summer snowflake, snakeshead fritillary, martagon lily, hellebore, pulmonaria, bleeding heart, columbine, foxglove, Solomon's seal, epimedium, astilbe, snakeroot, Japanese anemone, spiderwort, Siberian iris, daylily, and numerous hostas and primulas.

- Groundcovers are especially useful for shady spots, where it might be difficult for other plants to grow. When groundcovers are planted under trees, put in some early spring bulbs to pop up before the trees leaf out. There's a great selection of groundcovers with many good qualities — ajuga, lamium, pachysandra, vinca, and epimedium are just a few with interesting foliage that can add pizzazz to a forgotten shady corner.

- Spring ephemerals are wildflowers that bloom before deciduous trees leaf out, then die back in summer as shade becomes more dense. A lovely trio would be trillium with wood poppy and Virginia bluebell. For a more complete spring wildflower garden, add jack-in-the-pulpit, hepatica, and Virginia bluebells.

- Along with hostas, ferns make an invaluable contribution to the shade garden. Choose from numerous species, including lady fern, evergreen Christmas fern, hay-scented fern, shield fern, delicate maidenhair fern, Goldie's fern, cinnamon fern, and stunning Japanese painted fern.

For information on planting and amending the soil before planting, see the book in this series called *Care*.

With its beautifully marked fronds, Japanese painted fern (Athyrium niponicum *'Pictum') is a stunning additon to the shade garden.*

IN THE GARDEN CENTRE

Visiting the garden centre is always exciting — and for some people a little overwhelming. So much choice, so many colours, so many luscious plants to buy!

Sales statistics show that most people buy plants already in bloom. It's easy to understand why. Not only can you can see the plant's leaf shape and colour, but you can also see the beauty and colour of the blooms. Some lovely and valuable plants get overlooked, unfortunately, so we hope we've introduced you to some plants you might not see blooming in the garden centre.

Buying plants is a bit like grocery shopping. Make a list based on your needs and desires, and although you'll still let your heart take over now and then — which we also encourage! — you'll have your list to remind you of what you came to buy.

One of the most important aids in garden centres, other than knowledgeable staff, is the label that's attached to the plant. What does a good label tell you?

- the common name
- the botanical name
- description of the plant's features; information about flowering periods; some horticultural information
- use in landscape
- light requirements
- hardiness
- mature height and spread
- pruning information
- planting instructions

Read each label carefully to make sure you buy the plants that are right for your garden.

PLANTS FOR SUNNY SPOTS

TREES

Evergreens:
Cedar (*Thuja occidentalis*)
Fir (*Abies*)
Hemlock (*Tsuga*)
Juniper (*Juniperus*)
Larch (*Larix*)
Pine (*Pinus*)
Spruce (*Picea*)
Yew (*Taxus*)
Deciduous:
Ash (*Fraxinus*)
Ash, Mountain (*Sorbus*)
Beech (*Fagus*)
Birch (*Betula*)
Catalpa (*Catalpa*)
Ginkgo (*Ginkgo*)
Locust (*Robinia*)
Locust, Honey (*Gleditsia*)
Maple (*Acer*)
Oak (*Quercus*)
Olive, Russian (*Elaeagnus*)

SHRUBS

Evergreens:
Boxwood (*Buxus*)
Cedar (*Thuja occidentalis*)
Fir (*Abies*)
Juniper (*Juniperus*)
Pine (*Pinus*)
Rose Daphne (*Daphne cneorum*)
Spruce (*Picea*)
Yew (*Taxus*)

FLOWERING SHRUBS: see page 58

VINES

Clematis (*Clematis*)
Honeysuckle (*Lonicera*)
Kiwi (*Actinidia*)
Trumpet Vine (*Campsis*)
Wisteria (*Wisteria*)

PERENNIALS

Aster (*Aster*)
Aubrieta (*Aubrieta deltoides*)
Balloon Flower (*Platycodon grandiflorus*)
Basket of Gold (*Aurinia saxatilis*)
Bee Balm (*Monarda*)
Bellflower (*Campanula*)
Black-eyed Susan (*Rudbeckia*)
Blanket Flower (*Gaillardia*)
Chrysanthemum (*Chrysanthemum*)
Columbine (*Aquilegia*)
Coral bells (*Heuchera sanguinea*)
Coreopsis (*Coreopsis*)
Cranesbill (*Geranium*)
Daylily (*Hemerocallis*)
Delphinium (*Delphinium*)
Evening Primrose (*Oenothera*)
Flax (*Linum*)
Fleabane (*Erigeron*)
Globe Thistle (*Echinops*)
Goat's Beard (*Aruncus*)
Goldenrod (*Solidago*)
Iris (*Iris*)
Lady's Mantle (*Alchemilla*)
Lavender (*Lavandula*)
Lupine (*Lupinus*)
Mallow (*Malva*)
Maltese Cross (*Lychnis chalcedonica*)
Monkshood (*Aconitum*)

Oriental Poppy (*Papaver orientale*)
Peony (*Paeonia*)
Pink (*Dianthus*)
Purple Coneflower (*Echinacea purpurea*)
Red-hot Poker (*Kniphofia*)
Russian Sage (*Perovskia*)
Sea Holly (*Eryngium amethystinum*)
Sea Lavender (*Limonium*)
Snow in Summer (*Cerastium tomentosum*)
Speedwell (*Veronica*)
Spiderwort (*Tradescantia virginiana*)
Sun Rose (*Helianthemum*)
Thrift (*Armeria*)
Thyme (*Thymus*)
Yarrow (*Achillea*)

ANNUALS

Ageratum (*Ageratum*)
Black-eyed Susan Vine (*Thunbergia alata*)
*Canterbury Bell (*Campanula medium*)
Cockscomb (*Celosia*)
Coreopsis Annual (*Calliopsis*)
Cornflower (*Centaurea cyanus*)
Cosmos (*Cosmos*)
Cup and Saucer Plant (*Vine*) (*Cobaea scandens*)
*Daisy, English (*Bellis perennis*)

Dianthus(*Dianthus*)
Heliotrope (*Heliotropium arborescens*)
Marigold (*Calendula officinalis*)
Morning Glory (*Convolvulus tricolor*)
Moss Rose (*Portulaca grandiflora*)
Nasturtium (*Tropaeolum majus*)
Nicotiana (*Nicotiana*)
Petunia (*Petunia*)
Phlox (*Phlox drummondii*)
Poppy (*Papaver*)
Sea Lavender (*Limonium*)
Snapdragon (*Antirrhinum majus*)
Spiderflower (*Cleome hasslerana*)
Stock (*Matthiola incana*)
Swan River Daisy (*Brachycome iberidifolia*)
Sweet Alyssum (*Lobularia maritima*)
Sweet Pea(*Lathyrus odoratus*)
Verbena (*Verbena*)
Zinnia (*Zinnia*)

BULBS

Crocus (*Crocus*)
Daffodil (*Narcissus*)
Hyacinth (*Hyacinthus*)
Tulip (*Tulipa*)

*Biennials

PLANTS FOR SHADY SPOTS

TREES
Evergreens:
Cedar, White (*Thuja occidentalis*)
Cypress, Nootka False (*Chamaecyparis nootkatensis*)
Hemlock, Canadian (*Tsuga canadensis*)
Yew (*Taxus*)

Deciduous:
Katsura Tree (*Cercidiphyllum japonicum*)
Maple, Japanese (*Acer palmatum*)
Maple, Striped (*Acer pensylvanicum*)
Mountain Ash (*Sorbus aucuparia*)

SHRUBS
Evergreen:
Azalea (*Rhododendron*)
Boxwood (*Buxus*)
Euonymus (*Euonymus*)
Mountain Laurel (*Kalmia latifolia*)
Oregon Grape (*Mahonia*)
Rhododendron (*Rhododendron*)
Wintergreen (*Gaultheria*)
Deciduous:
Currant, Golden (*Ribes aureum*)
Dogwood (*Cornus*)
Elder (*Sambucus*)
Hydrangea (*Hydrangea*)
Kerria, Japanese (*Kerria japonica*)
Nannyberry (*Viburnum lentago*)
Serviceberry (*Amelanchier*)
Snowberry (*Symphoricarpos*)
Spiraea, False (*Sorbaria*)
Winterberry (*Ilex verticillata*)
Witch Hazel (*Hamamelis*)

VINES
Evergreen:
Akebia (*Akebia quinata*)
English Ivy (*Hedera helix*)
Euonymus (*Euonymus*)
Deciduous:
Climbing Hydrangea (*Hydrangea petiolaris*)
Kiwi (*Actinidia*)
Partridgeberry (*Mitchella repens*)
Porcelain Berry (*Ampelopsis brevipedunculata*)

PERENNIALS
Anemone, Japanese (*Anemone x hybrida*)
Astilbe (*Astilbe*)
Bear's Breech (*Acanthus mollis*)
Bellflower (*Campanula*)
Bergenia (*Bergenia*)
Bleeding Heart (*Dicentra*)
Cardinal Flower (*Lobelia cardinalis*)
Columbine (*Aquilegia*)
Coral bells (*Heuchera x brizoides*)
Corydalis (*Corydalis lutea*)
Cranesbill (*Geranium*)
Cyclamen (*Cyclamen*)
Daylily (*Hemerocallis*)
Dutchman's Breeches (*Dicentra cucullaria*)
Epimedium (*Epimedium*)
Ferns, in variety
Foamflower (*Tiarella*)
Foxglove (*Digitalis*)
Gentian (*Gentiana*)
Ginger, Wild (*Asarum*)
Goatsbeard (*Aruncus dioicus*)
Hellebore (*Helleborus*)
Hepatica (*Hepatica*)
Hosta (*Hosta*)
Iris, Siberian (*Iris sibirica*)
Jack-in-the-Pulpit (*Arisaema triphyllum*)
Lady's Mantle (*Alchemilla*)
Ligularia (*Ligularia stenocephala*)
Lily of the Valley (*Convallaria majalis*)
Lungwort (*Pulmonaria*)
Monkshood (*Aconitum*)
Nettle, Dead (*Lamium maculatum*)
Primrose (*Primula*)
Snakeroot (*Cimicifuga*)
Solomon's Seal (*Polygonatum*)
Spiderwort (*Tradescantia virginiana*)
Trillium (*Trillium grandiflorum*)

Virginia Bluebell (*Mertensia virginica*)
Woodruff, Sweet (*Galium odoratum*)

GROUNDCOVER
Evergreen:
Bugleweed (*Ajuga*)
Periwinkle (*Vinca*)
Spurge, Japanese (*Pachysandra*)

ANNUALS
Begonia, Wax (*Begonia x semperflorens-cultorum*)

Browallia (*Browallia*)
Caladium (*Caladium*)
Coleus (*Coleus*)
*Forget-me-not (*Myosotis sylvatica*)
Fuchsia (*Fuchsia*)
Impatiens (*Impatiens*)
Lobelia (*Lobelia*)
Polka-dot Plant (*Hypoestes phyllostachya*)

*Biennial

PLANTS FOR DAMP SOIL

TREES
Evergreen:
Cedar (*Thuja*)
Larch (*Larix*)
Deciduous:
Alder (*Alnus*)
Ash (*Fraxinus*)
Birch (*Betula*)
Cedar, White (*Thuja occidentalis*)
Hackberry (*Celtis occidentalis*)
Maple, Japanese (*Acer palmatum*)
Maple, Red (*Acer rubrum*)
Oak, Pin (*Quercus palustris*)
Poplar (*Populus*)
Willow (*Salix*)

SHRUBS
Bog Rosemary (*Andromeda polifolia*)
Dogwood, Red Osier (*Cornus sericea*)
Elderberry (*Sambucus canadensis*)
Highbush Cranberry (*Viburnum trilobum*)
St. Johnswort (*Hypericum*)

Summersweet (*Clethra alnifolia*)
Viburnum, Arrowwood (*Viburnum dentatum*)
Winterberry (*Ilex verticillata*)

PERENNIALS
Astilbe (*Astilbe*)
Bergenia (*Bergenia*)
Bleeding Heart (*Dicentra spectabilis*)
Bloodroot (*Sanguinaria canadensis*)
Bugleweed (*Ajuga reptans*)
Cardinal Flower (*Lobelia cardinalis*)
Columbine (*Aquilegia*)
Daylily (*Hemerocallis*)
Ferns, in variety
Filipendula (*Filipendula*)
Flag, Blue (*Iris versicolor*)
Flag, Yellow (*Iris pseudacorus*)
Globeflower (*Trollius*)
Hosta (*Hosta*)
Iris, Japanese (*Iris ensata*)
Iris, Siberian (*Iris sibirica*)
Jack-in-the-Pulpit (*Arisaema*)

Ligularia (*Ligularia stenocephala*)
Lily of the Valley (*Convallaria*)
Marsh Marigold (*Caltha palustris*)
Monkshood (*Aconitum*)
Obedient plant (*Physostegia*)
Primrose (*Primula*)
Rose Mallow (*Hibiscus moscheuf*)
Sedge (*Carex*)
Snakeroot, Black (*Cimifuga*)

Spiderwort (*Tradescantia virginiana*)
Sweet Woodruff (*Galium odoratum*)
Virginia Bluebell (*Mertensia virginica*)

BULBS
Camassia (*Camassia*)
Snake's head Fritillary (*Fritillaria meleagris angustifolia*)
Summer Snowflake (*Leucojum*)

PLANTS FOR DRY SOIL

TREES
Evergreens:
Juniper (*Juniperus*)
Deciduous:
Ash (*Fraxinus*)
Locust (*Robinia*)
Maple, Amur (*Acer ginnala*)
Mulberry (*Morus*)
Tree of Heaven (*Ailanthus altissima*)

SHRUBS
Evergreens:
Juniper (*Juniperus*)
Deciduous:
Bayberry (*Myrica pensylvanica*)
Beauty Bush (*Kolkwitzia amabilis*)
Butterfly Bush (*Buddleia davidii*)
Cinquefoil (*Potentilla*)
Firethorn (*Pyracantha*)
Flowering Quince (*Chaenomeles*)
Lavender (*Lavandula*)
Ninebark (*Physocarpus opulifolius*)
Pea Shrub (*Caragana*)
Privet (*Ligustrum*)
Rugosa Rose (*Rosa rugosa*)

Russian Olive (*Elaeagnus angustofolia*)
Sea Buckthorn (*Hippophae rhamnoides*)
Silverberry (*Eleagnus commutata*)
Sumac (*Rhus*)
Tamarisk (*Tamarix*)

VINES
Silver Lace Vine (*Polygonum aubertii*)
Wisteria (*Wisteria*)

PERENNIALS
Artemisia (*Artemisia*)
Beardtongue (*Penstemon*)
Blue Fescue (*Festuca ovina* 'Glauca')
Coreopsis (*Coreopsis*)
Evening Primrose (*Oenothera*)
Flax (*Linum*)
Gayfeather (*Liatris*)
Iris (*Iris x germanica*)
Lamb's Ears (*Stachys*)
Pink (*Dianthus*)
Prickly Pear (*Opuntia humifusa*)
Rock Cress (*Arabis*)
Russian Sage (*Perovskia*)
Sage (*Salvia*)

Snow-in-Summer (*Cerastium tomentosum*)
Stonecrop (*Sedum*)
Sunrose (*Helianthemum nummularium*)
Yarrow (*Achillea*)
Yucca (*Yucca*)

ANNUALS
African Daisy (*Arctotis*)
Alyssum (*Alyssum maritima*)
Moss Rose (*Portulaca grandiflora*)
Nasturtium (*Tropaeolum majus*)
Poppy, California (*Eschscholzia californica*)

PLANTS WITH COLOURFUL BERRIES, CONES OR FRUIT

TREES
Evergreen:
Korean Fir (*Abies koreana*)
Deciduous:
Ash, Mountain (*Sorbus*)
Crab Apple, Flowering (*Malus*)
Hawthorn (*Crataegus*)

SHRUBS
Evergreen:
Cotoneaster (*Cotoneaster*)
Firethorn (*Pyracantha*)
Holly (*Ilex*)
Oregon Grape (*Mahonia*)
Wintergreen (*Gaultheria*)
Deciduous:
Bayberry (*Myrica pensylvanica*)
Beauty Bush (*Kolkwitzia amabilis*)
Buffaloberry, Silver (*Shepherdia*)
Chokeberry (*Aronia*)
Cotoneaster (*Cotoneaster*)

Dogwood (*Cornus*)
Elderberry (*Sambucus*)
Firethorn (*Pyracantha*)
Honeysuckle (*Lonicera*)
Rugosa Rose (*Rosa rugosa*)
Sea Buckthorn (*Hippophae rhamnoides*)
Serviceberry (*Amelanchier*)
Snowberry (*Symphoricarpos*)
Staghorn Sumac (*Rhus typhina*)
Viburnum (*Viburnum*)
Winterberry (*Ilex verticillata*)

VINES
Bittersweet (*Celastrus scandens*)
Porcelain Berry (*Ampelopsis brevipedunculata*)

ANNUALS
Chinese Lantern (*Physalis alkekengi*)
Gourd, Ornamental (*Cucurbita pepo*)
Honesty (*Lunaria*)

TREES AND SHRUBS WITH ATTRACTIVE BLOOMS

Almond, Flowering (*Prunus*)
Beauty Bush (*Kolkwitzia amabilis*)
Butterfly Bush (*Buddleia*)

Caryopteris (*Caryopteris*)
Cherry, Flowering (*Prunus*)
Cinquefoil (*Potentilla*)

Crab Apple, Flowering (*Malus*)
Currant, Flowering (*Ribes*)
Daphne (*Daphne*)
Deutzia (*Deutzia*)
Dogwood, Flowering (*Cornus*)
False Spiraea (*Sorbaria*)
Forsythia (*Forsythia*)
Hawthorn (*Crataegus*)
Heather (*Erica*)
Hydrangea (*Hydrangea*)
Kerria (*Kerria*)
Lilac (*Syringa*)
Magnolia (*Magnolia*)

Mock Orange (*Philadelphus*)
Mountain Laurel (*Kalmia latifolia*)
Pear, Ornamental (*Pyrus*)
Quince, Flowering (*Chaenomeles*)
Rhododendron (*Rhododendron*)
Rose of Sharon (*Hibiscus syriacus*)
Serviceberry (*Amelanchier*)
Shrub Roses, in variety
Spiraea (*Spiraea*)
Summersweet (*Clethra*)
Tamarisk (*Tamarix*)
Viburnum (*Viburnum*)
Weigela (*Weigela*)

SOME PERENNIALS AND BULBS FOR SEASONAL FLOWERING

SPRING:
Basket of Gold (*Aurinia saxatilis*)
Bleeding Heart (*Dicentra spectabilis*)
Candytuft (*Iberis sempervirens*)
Columbine (*Aquilegia*)
Crocus (*Crocus*)
Daffodil (*Narcissus*)
Hellebore (*Helleborus*)
Hyacinth (*Hyacinthus*)
Iris (*Iris*)
Leopard's Bane (*Doronicum*)
Moss Pink (*Phlox subulata*)
Pasque Flower (*Pulsatilla*)
Peony (*Paeonia*)
Poppy, Oriental (*Papaver orientalis*)
Primrose (*Primula*)
Pyrethrum (*Tanacetum coccineum*)
Rockcress (*Arabis*)
Thrift (*Armeria*)
Tulip (*Tulipa*)

SUMMER
Astilbe (*Astilbe*)
Coreopsis (*Coreopsis*)
Daylily (*Hemerocallis*)
Delphinium (*Delphinium*)
Flax (*Linum*)
Foxglove (*Digitalis*)
Gas Plant (*Dictamnus albus*)
Geum (*Geum*)
Gladiolus (*Gladiolus*)
Globeflower (*Trollius*)
Golden Margeurite (*Anthemis*)
Hollyhock (*Alcea rosea*)
Maltese cross (*Lychnis*)
Pink (*Dianthus*)
Shasta Daisy (*Leucanthemum x superbum*)
Yarrow (*Achillea*)

LATE SUMMER, EARLY FALL
Anemone, Japanese (*Anemone x hybrida*)
Black-eyed Susan (*Rudbeckia*)

Chrysanthemum (*Chrysanthemum*)
Aster (*Aster*)
Heliopsis (*Heliopsis*)
Purple coneflower (*Echinacea*)
Rose Mallow (*Hibiscus*)

Showy Stonecrop (*Sedum spectabile*)

BULBS
Fall-flowering Crocus (*Colchicum*)
Cyclamen (*Cyclamen*)

TREES AND SHRUBS FOR SMALL SPACES

Ash, Upright European Mountain
  (*Sorbus aucuparia* 'Fastigiata')
Beauty Bush (*Kolkwitzia amabilis*)
Cinquefoil (*Potentilla*)
Crab Apple, Columnar (*Malus*
  'Adirondack')
Dogwood, Kousa (*Cornus kousa*)
Ginkgo, Pyramidal (*Ginkgo*
  'Fairmount', 'Lakeview', or 'Mayfield')

Maple, Columnar Norway (*Acer
  platanoides* 'Columnare' or 'Erectum')
Maple, Crimson Sentry (*Acer
  platanoides* 'Crimson Sentry')
Mountain Laurel (*Kalmia latifolia*)
Oak, Pyramidal English (*Quercus robur*
  'Fastigiata')
Pear, Callery (*Pyrus calleryana*
  'Capital')

TREES AND SHRUBS FOR HEDGING AND WINDBREAKS

Evergreen:
Cedar (*Thuja occidentalis*)
Cedar, Red (*Thuja plicata*)
Cypress, False (*Chamaecyparis*)
Holly (*Ilex*)
Juniper (*Juniperus*)
Pine (*Pinus*)
Spruce, Norway (*Picea abies*)
Yew (*Taxus*)
Deciduous:
Barberry, Japanese (*Berberis thunbergii*)
Bayberry (*Myrica pensylvanica*)
Beech, European (*Fagus sylvatica*)
Cinquefoil (*Potentilla*)
Cotoneaster (*Cotoneaster*)
Firethorn (*Pyracantha*)

Hawthorn (*Crataegus monogyna*)
Honeysuckle (*Lonicera nitida*)
Hornbeam, European (*Carpinus
  betulus*)
Lombardy Poplar (*Populus nigra*
  'Italica')
Privet (*Ligustrum*)
Quince, Flowering (*Chaenomeles*)
Rugosa Rose (*Rosa Rugosa*)
Russian Olive (*Elaeagnus angustifolia*)
Saskatoon (*Amelanchier alnifolia*)
Sea Buckthorn (*Hippophae rhamnoides*)
Siberian Peashrub (*Caragana
  arborescens*)
Snowberry (*Symphoricarpos albus*)
Tamarisk (*Tamarix*)

PLANTS WITH COLOURFUL FOLIAGE

TREES

Evergreens:

Any juniper described as "blue"

Any spruce described as "blue"

Deciduous:

Ash (*Sorbus*)

Beech, Copper (*Fagus sylvatica* 'Purpurea')

Crab Apple, Royalty (*Malus purpurea* 'Royalty')

*Ginkgo (*Ginkgo*)

*Katsura Tree (*Cercidiphyllum japonicum*)

*Maple (*Acer*)

*Mountain Ash (*Sorbus*)

*Pear, Ornamental (*Pyrus Calleryana*)

Sand Cherry, Purpleleaf (*Prunus cistena*)

Serviceberry, Downy (*Amelanchier arborea*)

SHRUBS

Evergreens:

Any juniper described as "blue" (such as 'Blue Rug')

Any juniper described as "gold" (such as 'Gold Star')

'Canadale Gold' Euonymus (gold) (*Euonymus*)

Golden Japanese Yew (gold) (*Taxus cuspidata* 'Aurescens')

Deciduous:

Buffaloberry, Silver (*Shepherdia argentea*)

*Burning Bush, (*Euonymus alata*)

*Currant, Flowering (*Ribes*)

Dogwood, Yellowtwig (*Cornus stolonifera* 'Flaviramea')

Highbush Cranberry (*Viburnum opulus*)

*Maple, Amur (*Acer ginnala*)

Maple, Bloodgood Japanese (*Acer palmatum* 'Bloodgood')

Maple, Purple Japanese (*Acer palmatum* 'Atropurpureum')

Mock Orange, Golden (*Philadelphus coronarius* 'Aureus')

Nannyberry (*Viburnum lentago*)

Ninebark, Golden (*Physocarpus opulifolius* 'Dart's Golden')

Olive, Russian (*Elaeagnus*)

Privet, Vicary Golden (*Ligustrum vicaryi*)

*Serviceberry (*Amelanchier*)

Smoketree, Purple (*Cotinus coggygria* 'Purpureus')

*Sumac (*Rhus*)

Weigela, Variegated (*Weigela florida* 'Variegata')

*Witch Hazel (*Hamamelis*)

VINES

Boston Ivy (*Part henociss*)

*Virginia Creeper (*Parthenocissus quinquefolia*)

*Foliage turns colour in autumn

PLANTS FOR GROUNDCOVER

SHRUBS
Evergreen:
Bearberry (*Arctostaphylos uva-ursi*)
Cotoneaster (*Cotoneaster*)
English Ivy (*Hedera helix*)
Euonymus (*Euonymus fortunei*)
Juniper, 'Bar Harbour' (*Juniperus horizontalis* 'Bar Habrour')
Juniper, 'Blue Chip' (*J. horizontalis* 'Blue chip')
Juniper, 'Blue Mat' (*J. horizontalis* 'Blue Mat')
Juniper, 'Prince of Wales' (*J. horizontalis* 'Prince of Wales')
Deciduous:
False Spiraea (*Sorbaria*)
Honeysuckle, Morrow (*Lonicera morrowii*)
Japanese Spurge (*Pachysandra*)
Periwinkle (*Vinca*)
Stephanandra (*Stephanandra*)
Sumac, Fragrant (*Rhus aromatica*)

PERENNIALS
Basket of Gold (*Aurinia saxatilis*)

Bugleweed (*Ajuga reptans*)
Candytuft (*Iberis*)
Cinquefoil (*Potentilla*)
Cranesbill Geranium (*Geranium*)
Crown Vetch (*Coronilla varia*)
Dead Nettle (*Lamium*)
Epimedium (*Epimedium*)
Evening Primrose (*Oenothera*)
Gout Weed (*Aegopodium podagraria*)
Lambs' Ears (*Stachys byzantina*)
Lily of the Valley (*Convallaria majalis*)
Moss Pink (*Phlox subulata*)
Rockcress (*Arabis*)
Snow-in-Summer (*Cerastium tomentosum*)
Soapwort (*Saponaria*)
Stonecrop (*Sedum*)
Sunrose (*Helianthemum nummularium*)
Sweet Woodruff (*Galium odoratum*)
Thyme (*Thymus*)
Virginia Creeper (*Parthenocissus quinquefolia*)
Wild Ginger (*Asarum*)

SHADE TREES

Ash (*Fraxinus*)
Ash, Mountain (*Sorbus*)
Beech (*Fagus*)
Locust, Honey (*Gleditsia*)

Maple, Norway (*Acer platanoides*, especially 'Deborah' and Crimson King')
Maple, Red (*Acer rubrum*)
Maple, Sugar (*Acer saccharum*)
Oak (*Quercus*)

TREES AND SHRUBS FOR CLAY SOIL

TREES
Evergreens:
Euonymus (*Euonymus*)
Juniper (*Juniperus*)
Pine, Austrian (*Pinus nigra*)
Spruce, Colorado (*Picea pungens*)
Spruce, White (*Picea glauca*)
Deciduous:
Ash (*Fraxinus*)
Ash, Mountain (*Sorbus*)
Catalpa (*Catalpa*)
Crab Apple (*Malus*)
Locust, Honey (*Gleditsia*)
Maple, Norway (*Acer platanoides*)
Poplar (*Populus*)
Sycamore (*Platanus occidentalis*)
Willow (*Salix*)

SHRUBS
Crab Apple (*Malus*)
Dogwood (*Cornus*)
Euonymus (*Euonymus*)
Forsythia (*Forsythia*)
Honeysuckle (*Lonicera*)
Magnolia (*Magnolia*)
Pea Shrub (*Caragana*)
Russian Olive (*Elaeagnus angustifolia*)
Serviceberry (*Amelanchier*)
Spirea (*Spiraea*)

PLANTS THAT TOLERATE SALT AND SEASIDE CONDITIONS

TREES
Evergreen:
Cedar (*Thuja occidentalis*)
Pine (*Pinus*)
Deciduous:
Maple, Norway (*Acer planatoides*)

SHRUBS
Bayberry (*Myrica pensylvanica*)
Bearberry (*Arctostaphylos uva-ursi*)
Rhododendron (*Rhododendron*)
Rugosa Rose (*Rosa rugosa*)

VINES
Bittersweet (*Celastrus scandens*)
English Ivy (*Hedera helix*)

PERENNIALS
Showy Stonecrop (*Sedum*)
Yarrow (*Achillea*)

ANNUALS
Dusty Miller (*Senecio cineraria*)
Dwarf Marigold (*Tagetes tenuifolia*)
Petunia (*Petunia*)

BULBS
Daffodil (*Narcissus*)

INDEX

ISBN: 0-9697259-2-2

Produced for Loblaws Inc. by Alpha Corporation/Susan Yates, Publisher
Written for Loblaws Inc. by Wendy Thomas and Janet Davis
Landscape design consultant and horticultural expert: Janet Rosenberg
Photographs and horticultural editing: Janet Davis
Photographs by Sharon Kish: p 3, 4, 7, 11, 13, 17, 19, 21, 23, 33, 39, inside back cover
Copy editor: Greg Ioannou/Colborne Communications
Text and cover design: Dave Murphy/ArtPlus Ltd.
Page layout: Leanne Knox/ArtPlus Ltd.
Printed and bound in Canada by Kromar Printing

GARDEN DESIGN CREDITS

page 3, 4, 7: Janet Rosenberg & Associates; page 8: Neil Turnbull; page 11: Janet Rosenberg & Associates; page 15: Judith Kennedy; page 17, 19, 21, 22, 33, 39: Janet Rosenberg & Associates; page 41: Design by Allen Haskell; page 45: Spadina Historic House & Gardens; page 47: Butchart Gardens; page 49: Ted Johnston; page 51: Rosemary Pauer; inside back cover: Janet Rosenberg & Associates